Philip Melanchthon and the Lutheran Confession of Eucharistic Sacrifice

Rev. D. Richard Stuckwisch, M.Div., S.T.M., Ph.D.
Pastor, Emmaus Ev. Lutheran Church,
South Bend, Indiana

• Repristination Press •

First Edition: 1997
Second Edition: 2011

Repristination Press
P.O. Box 173
Bynum, Texas 76631

www.repristinationpress.com

ISBN-10 1-891469-33-9
ISBN-13 978-1891469336

Introduction

The *eucharistic sacrifice* is not alien to Lutheranism, but neither is it commonly discussed. It exists as a legitimate aspect of Lutheran doctrine, but one that rarely appears at any level of catechesis. Appropriately, the notion of Christian sacrifice does surface at times in the context of the Church's liturgical worship. But apart from any doctrinal instruction, even these doxological references are open to ambiguity and confusion. Each believer is left to think of sacrifice as seems right in his or her own eyes. As with terms like *catholic* and *evangelical, sacrifice* has been omitted from common parlance, along with its orthodox theology.

Such neglect of the eucharistic sacrifice has had consequences. For example, it has no doubt contributed to false concepts of "worship," which emphasize "celebration" without regard for the painful Theology of the Cross. Not that Lutherans are averse to *celebration* — but in this life it is always in, with, and under the Cross. Our Christian life begins with a dying and rising with Christ in Baptism. And at the very heart and center of the Church's life and worship, we *celebrate* the Lord's Supper as a proclamation of His *death* until He comes. Thus, if we are to celebrate with Him, we must also die with Him. This Theology of the Cross is at the heart of the eucharistic sacrifice.

A neglect of the eucharistic sacrifice is perhaps also to blame for the infrequent use of the Lord's Supper in generations past. For a pietistic fear of unworthy participation is itself a departure from the eucharistic sacrifice. To fear that we are unworthy of the Lord's Supper is to evaluate ourselves on the basis of our own works and merit, and to view our sin as greater than the crucified Body and shed Blood of Christ. On the other hand, to approach the Altar with a eucharistic sacrifice is to acknowledge our unworthiness as very great indeed, and yet to come nonetheless with a broken and contrite heart, clinging to the mercy and forgiveness of Christ. That Christian is truly worthy and well-prepared who believes these words, "given and shed *for you,* for the forgiveness of sins." Such belief is the eucharistic sacrifice. It is the very opposite of fear.

In an effort to overcome the neglect of the past, this essay will attempt to articulate a Lutheran theology of the eucharistic sacrifice as it was taught and confessed especially by Philip Melanchthon. It will demonstrate that eucharistic sacrifice, properly understood, is an essential aspect of true Lutheran worship and a proper celebration of the Lord's Supper. In fact, this sacrifice encompasses the whole panorama of worship. Simply stated, it consists of repentance and faith, which always express themselves in prayer and thanksgiving. Apart from this eucharistic sacrifice, we are left with one form or another of the Roman sacrificial Mass. Thus, Eucharist or Mass; or, in more familiar terms, the religion of the Gospel *vs.* the religion of the Law. It is one or the other, but never both. In the words of Dr. Luther:

> The true mass and the true priesthood have fallen and have been completely eradicated, so that instead of faith they have preached outward works, which even a sinner and rogue can do. The fruit and the power of the true, genuine sacrifice is suppressed and exterminated, so that no one cares to endure or bear the cross.... Hence the glory and honor of the true priesthood is extinguished

and in its stead an idol of human law and human doctrine is set up.[1]

I. Lutheran Objections to the Sacrifice of the Mass

Already in the controversy over Indulgences, the catalyst of the Reformation, Luther rejected the notion of a benefit *ex opere operato* ("by the outward act") in the Sacraments.[2] He commonly referred to the phrase, *not the Sacrament, but faith in the Sacrament, justifies*. That is to say, faith must precede and accompany reception of the Sacraments, in order to receive the benefits that are truly offered and bestowed in these Means of Grace. Luther's view thus contradicted the common (*de facto*) understanding and practice of the Sacraments in his day.

With respect to the Sacrament of the Altar, priests were attempting by a supposed "sacrifice of the Mass" to achieve atonement and earn the forgiveness of sins. Luther opposed this sacrificial understanding of the Mass for the same reason he opposed the doctrine of justification by works. In either case, the Christian is required to *earn* his or her salvation from God, whereas the Christian life for

1 *Luther's Works*, American Edition, Fifty-Five Volumes (LW), ed. Pelikan and Lehmann (St. Louis and Minneapolis, 1955–1986) 36:161 (1521)

2 "Since the thirteenth century *ex opere operato* ('by the mere performance,' or 'by the outward act') was a formula customarily applied to the sacraments, which were said to be efficacious if the recipient did not interpose an obstacle and if he had what the Augsburg Confession and the Apology call 'historical faith,' i.e., assent rather than trust." (Tappert: 115n8)

Melanchthon remarks in Ap.IV:"Nowhere can our opponents say how the Holy Spirit is given. They imagine that the sacraments bestow the Holy Spirit *ex opere operato* without the proper attitude in the recipient, as though the gift of the Holy Spirit were a minor matter." (Tappert: 115, Ap.IV [63])

Luther is always a reception of the gracious forgiveness of God by faith. Thus, Luther's concern was not so much that Christ is supposedly re–sacrificed in the Mass; his foremost criticism was leveled against the attempt to offer *any sacrifice for sin at all.* Salvation is found in Christ alone, on account of His historically–grounded, once–for–all, sacrificial death on the Cross, where He suffered (*as God*) the entire wrath of God against sin and endured the punishments of hell itself in our place; for His sake alone, Atonement has already been achieved and established, for all people and every sin, everywhere and for all time, and God has already been reconciled to the world. "The mass will not then be a sacrifice brought by human beings to God — even if it is Christ that they think they are sacrificing. . . . The mass must be placed under the sign of the promise, and not under that of a work or a sacrifice."[3]

Luther's younger protégée, Philip Melanchthon, likewise identified the chief problem of the sacrificial Mass with the notion of a work performed to earn forgiveness. As he writes in the Apology:

> Our opponents have collected many statements to prove that the Mass is a sacrifice. But all the quotations from the Fathers and the arguments they adduce are silenced by the fact that the Mass does not confer grace *ex opere operato,* nor merit for others the forgiveness of venial

3 Marc Lienhard, *Luther: Witness to Jesus Christ,* tr. Edwin Robertson (Minneapolis, 1982): 130. Cf. LW 36:169 (1521); also, Vilmos Vajta, *Luther on Worship: An Interpretation,* tr. U. S. Leupold (Philadelphia, 1958): 34*ff*. For a more nuanced description of Luther's two–fold opposition to the Mass (as a *work*, and as a *sacrifice*), *cf.* Carl Wisløff, *The Gift of Communion: Luther's Controversy with Rome on Eucharistic Sacrifice,* tr. Joseph Shaw (Minneapolis, 1964): 41–72.

> or mortal sins, of guilt, or of punishment. This single answer refutes all our opponents' objections, both here in the Confutation and in all their other books about the Mass. (Tappert: 250, Ap.XXIV [9])

Even earlier, Melanchthon had already staked out the evangelical Lutheran position in the Augsburg Confession (AC). There we see most clearly the point of conflict in the sacrifice of the Mass.

> St. Paul taught that we obtain grace before God through faith and not through works. Manifestly contrary to this teaching is the misuse of the Mass by those who think that grace is obtained through the performance of this work. . . . The holy sacrament was not instituted to make provision for a sacrifice for sin — for the sacrifice has already taken place — but to awaken our faith and comfort our consciences when we perceive that through the sacrament grace and forgiveness of sin are promised us by Christ. (Tappert: 59, AC XXIV [28])

By way of contrast, Melanchthon comments on the prevailing attitude of his day:

> It was taught that our Lord Christ had by his death made satisfaction only for original sin, and had instituted the Mass as a sacrifice for other sins. This transformed the Mass into a sacrifice for the living and the dead, a sacrifice by means of which sin was taken away and God was reconciled. Thereupon followed a debate as to whether one Mass held for many people merited as much as a special Mass held for an individual. Out of this grew the countless multiplication of Masses, by performance of which men expected to get everything needed from

> God. Meanwhile faith in Christ and true service of God were forgotten. (Tappert: 58, AC XXIV [21])

Actually, it is difficult to say with any certainty, whether "the official teaching of the Roman Church was precisely what the reformers stated." But most scholars today will readily admit that the practice of the Church, the typical understanding of the Mass and of indulgences, and "the rather common preaching and teaching in this line," often with ecclesiastical approval, "did present cause for concern."[4]

As part of its concerted response to the Reformation, the Council of Trent (1545–1563) first dealt specifically with the sacrifice of the Mass in 1547. The same topic was taken up again when the Council reconvened in 1552, and then again in 1562. Throughout these protracted discussions, the theologians and bishops agreed, that "the Mass is a sacramental or symbolic reenactment of the Cross. It is not a *re–presentation*; it is rather a representing of the sacrifice of the Cross." Yet, "the Mass is no mere commemoration, but a sacrifice." It is truly an "immolation" because it is an image of the Passion which, "by the intention of Christ," represents "the sacrifice of the Cross."[5]

Now, in the Apology, Melanchthon had spelled out very clearly a distinction between the Christian's proper sacrifice of thanksgiving and a propitiatory sacrifice for sin. As he explains:

---

4 Kenan Osborne, *The Christian Sacraments of Initiation: Baptism, Confirmation, Eucharist* (New York, 1987): 215

5 James T. O'Connor, *The Hidden Manna: A Theology of the Eucharist* (San Francisco, 1988): 228ff.

> There are two, and only two, basic types of sacrifice. One is the propitiatory sacrifice; this is a work of satisfaction for guilt and punishment that reconciles God or placates his wrath or merits the forgiveness of sins for others. The other type is the eucharistic sacrifice; this does not merit the forgiveness of sins or reconciliation, but by it those who have been reconciled give thanks or show their gratitude for the forgiveness of sins and other blessings received. (Tappert: 252, Ap.XXIV [19])

With this distinction in mind, it is clear what the Council of Trent meant when it defined the Eucharist as sacrifice. For the Council declares quite pointedly in its twenty–second session:

> [Third Canon]: If anyone says that the sacrifice of the mass is one only of praise and thanksgiving; or that it is a mere commemoration of the sacrifice consumated on the cross but not a propitiatory one; or that it profits him only who receives, and ought not to be offered for the living and the dead, for sins, punishments, satisfactions, and other necessities, let him be anathema.[6]

Thankfully, the Lutheran theologian Martin Chemnitz (a protégée in turn of Melanchthon) provides a careful Examination of Trent, from the perspective of one of the Council's primary targets.[7] He begins a consideration of the Mass by noting the need for a clear understanding of just exactly what is being called a "sacrifice" in the Eucharist. In his own answer to that question, Chemnitz points out repeatedly

---

6 *The Canons and Decrees of the Council of Trent*, tr. H. J. Schroeder (Rockford, IL: Tan Books, 1978): 149

7 *Cf.* Martin Chemnitz, *Examination of the Council of Trent, Part II (Ex)*, tr. F. Kramer (St. Louis, 1978): 439ff.

that the many and great benefits described by the Council — "divine grace, forgiveness of sins," *etc.* — "are not ascribed to Communion but to the sacrifice of the Mass" (Chemnitz, Ex: 450). Thus, for example, the Council of Trent was able to treat "the Mystery of the Eucharist as sacrifice" several years *after* it had already completed its canons and decrees on "the Eucharist as Sacrament" (O'Connor: 226). For the Roman Catholics, these two aspects of the Eucharist were two separate issues.

According to the Lutherans, and contrary to the teaching of Trent, the Church does nothing in the Lord's Supper to *earn* grace and forgiveness; she only *receives* what Christ has already earned for her. What is more, there can be no grace conferred in the Eucharist *ex opere operato,* that is, apart from faith, much less apart from the actual eating and drinking! But in fact, the Roman Mass had caused the Sacrament itself to be neglected, for despite all the daily Masses being offered, few people were receiving the Body and Blood of Christ on a regular basis. "Whereas Christ instituted the use of His Supper for all who receive it, who take, eat, and drink, the papalist Mass transfers the use and benefit of the celebration of the Lord's Supper . . . to the onlookers, who do not communicate, yes, to those who are absent, and even to the dead" (Chemnitz, Ex: 498).

Clearly, then, from the Lutheran perspective, the sacrifice of the Mass was nothing less than a rejection of the ancient Christian truth. For it is "an extraordinary perversion . . . to make a sacrifice out of a sacrament, in the way the papalists speak of their Mass, namely, that the representatory action of the priest procures for us the application of the benefits of Christ and that anyone who causes a Mass to be celebrated in his behalf by this work procures grace and whatever other things are ascribed to the Mass" (Chemnitz, Ex: 498). The Lutherans perceived at this point a virtual denial of the Cross of Christ, as well as the clearest manifestation of works righteousness.

Opposition to this sacrificial Mass and to the notion of "*ex opere operato*" is the consistent position of the Lutheran Confessions. As early as AC III, Christ is said to be "a sacrifice not only for original sin but also for all other sins" (Tappert: 54, AC III [3]). And the benefits of this once–for–all sacrifice of Christ are received by faith alone. Thus Melanchthon writes in his *Loci Communes* of 1543 (LC43):

> We must reject the error of the monks and the sacrificing priests, who devise the idea that by the mere doing of the work (*ex opere operato*), as they say, the reception is of benefit without any good intention on our part. From where have these Pharisaic ravings entered the church? It clearly says [Rom. 1:17], "The just shall live by his faith." Therefore in the reception of the Sacrament it is necessary to add faith, which is thinking of many very important matters, such as the wrath of God against sin; the death of the Son of God, by which the Father is reconciled; and the giving of the Gospel and the Sacraments, by which He applies to us the promised remission of sins. For the Sacraments apply the promise to individuals. (LC43: 148)[8]

8 Already in 1521, Melanchthon had written clearly: "There is only one sacrifice, only one satisfaction. That is Christ. Beyond him there is none other. . . . So we offer up nothing when we participate in the table of the Lord. . . . Just as each man is baptized for himself, so each man partakes at the table

It is never the case for the Lutherans that the Sacrament is a worthless or empty thing apart from faith, but only that the benefits truly offered and bestowed must be received by faith alone. Thus, as already indicated, there can be no grace conferred in the Lord's Supper apart from faith. That is the first and foremost objection to the sacrifice of the Mass. Furthermore, the Mass is not a sacrifice for sin, because the very thing that faith receives is the forgiveness that has already been achieved by the one, eternal Sacrifice of Christ upon the Cross. In short, the Lutheran Confessors leave no room for even the slightest accommodation of the sacrificial Mass. It is the very opposite of the Gospel. And yet, as we shall hear, these very same Lutherans have no objection to a proper understanding of sacrifice, that is, of *eucharistic sacrifice*. Indeed, *this* sacrifice permeates the heart of Lutheran theology. What is more, the rejection of the Roman Mass was simultaneously a return to the true eucharistic sacrifice.

II. Definitions and Distinctions

In light of the abuses surrounding the Mass, the Augsburg Confession avoided the use of sacrificial language, especially in the context of the Lord's Supper. The Roman Catholic theologians recognized this omission for what it

---

for himself. He rightly partakes who uses it as a sign to confirm his faith. He sins who partakes with the idea of offering up something unto God." (Melanchthon, *Propositions on the Mass*: 65). In 1555, he was still saying essentially the same: "This error, that the priest's sacrifice merits forgiveness of sins for himself or others, living or dead, obviously contradicts the article of faith that we have forgiveness only through faith and trust in Christ, as this passage clearly says, 'The just live by faith' [cf. Rom. 1:17]" (Melanchthon, *On Christian Doctrine: Loci Communes 1555* [LC55]: 221).

was — an implicit denial of their Eucharistic doctrine — and they responded accordingly with much polemical defense of their Mass. Their arguments only serve to confuse the matter, however, because the Roman Confutation of the Augsburg Confession uses Old Testament texts alongside the New Testament without distinction.[9]

> The Confutation has a great deal to say about sacrifice, though in our Confession we purposely avoided this term because of its ambiguity. . . .[10] For the last ten years our opponents have been publishing almost endless books about sacrifice, but none of them has defined it. (Tappert: 251, Ap.XXIV [14])

In retrospect, it might have been wiser for the Lutherans to work from the start at recapturing a Biblical understanding of sacrifice, instead of trying to avoid the term. The Book of Hebrews, for example, after proving that the Sacrifice of Christ had brought an end to Levitical sacrifices,

---

9 Cf. Holsten Fagerberg, *A New Look at the Lutheran Confessions (1529–1537)*, tr. G. Lund (St. Louis, 1972): 202–203

10 As Chemnitz also explains:

> We prefer that the Lord's Supper should be called a sacrament rather than a sacrifice. For first, Scripture, which is able to give things the most correct and fitting names of all, nowhere calls the Lord's Supper a sacrifice. Second, the name "sacrifice" obscures the true doctrine and use of the Lord's Supper more than a little. For a sacrifice is an action by which we give or offer something to God. However, Christ instituted the Lord's Supper that in it (as is the nature of sacraments) He might deal with us — giving, offering, applying and sealing with the pledge of His body and blood the merits of His passion. . . . The term "sacrifice," however, leads us away from these things and to what we, in the action of the Lord's Supper, offer and give to God. . . . Third, the theatrical sacrifice of the papalist Mass . . . shows sufficiently what trouble the improper terms denoting sacrifice cause when they are applied to the Lord's Supper. (Chemnitz, Ex: 492–493)

goes on to say that we should offer up a "*sacrifice* of praise to God" (Hebrews 13:15). Surely, then, there was no need to abandon the term even in the midst of violent controversy. Indeed, it is possible and even necessary to define what a sacrifice is and to understand its place in the Christian life.

Thus, in the Apology, Melanchthon takes a new approach. Here he does not dismiss the language of sacrifice in his discussion of the Lord's Supper, but makes an effort to remove the ambiguity and confusion.[11] To this end, he begins with definitions and distinctions of the terms *sacrament* and *sacrifice*:

> The theologians make a proper distinction between sacrament and sacrifice. The genus common to both could be "ceremony" or "sacred act." A sacrament is a ceremony or act in which God offers us the content of the promise joined to the ceremony.... By way of contrast, a sacrifice is a ceremony or act which we render to God to honor him. (Tappert: 252, Ap.XXIV [17])[12]

11 "Now, lest we plunge blindly into this business, we must indicate, in the first place, a distinction as to what is, and what is not, a sacrifice. To know this is expedient and good for all Christians" (Concordia Triglotta: 389, Ap.XXIV [16]).

12 Melanchthon describes this difference again in his *Loci* of 1543:

> Although it seems childish to distinguish between the words "sacrament" and "sacrifice," yet the situation demands that in religious ceremonies the difference be observed and boundaries defined. Some ceremonies are signs and notices of promises in which God shows something to us; but other ceremonies are not properly the signs of promise, but works which we render to God. . . . Since the words "sacrament" and "sacrifice" are in common use, we shall retain them also. Thus a sacrament is a ceremony which is a sign of a promise whereby God promises or shows something to us. . . . A sacrifice is a ceremony or work of ours which we render to God so that we honor Him, that is, we bear witness that we acknowledge

Melanchthon then continues with the most important distinction in his treatment of sacrifice: The propitiatory sacrifice is a work that reconciles God or merits the forgiveness of sins. The eucharistic sacrifice does not merit the forgiveness of sins or reconciliation, but by it those who have been reconciled give thanks for the forgiveness of sins and other blessings received (*cf.* Tappert: 252, Ap.XXIV [19]). He provides a more detailed distinction of the two types of sacrifice in his *Loci Communes*:

> There are two kinds of sacrifice which are very similar to one another, and there are no others. There is the propitiatory sacrifice, that is, a work which merits for some the remission of guilt and eternal punishment, or a work which reconciles God and placates the wrath of God on behalf of some people and is a means of satisfaction for sin and eternal punishment. The second kind of sacrifice is the eucharistic sacrifice which does not merit the remission of sins or reconciliation, but comes from those who have been reconciled, so that we give thanks to God for the remission of sins which we have received and for His other benefits, or we return thanks by means of our obedience. This distinction can be clearly shown from the Epistle to the Hebrews [10:1–18] which teaches that there was only one propitiatory sacrifice made in the world. Therefore, there remain all the other works in which those who have been reconciled must demonstrate their obedience. (LC43: 151)

Unfortunately, when people think or speak of *sacrifice,* they usually have in mind a sacrifice of propitiation.

---

that He to whom we give obedience is the true God, and for this reason do we render this obedience. (LC43: 150)

Therein lies the source of confusion. The Scriptures, on the other hand — except for descriptions of the Cross — speak most often of the eucharistic sacrifice. Thus, for example, Melanchthon describes the sacrifice of Abel in terms of faith:

> By faith Abel offered a more acceptable sacrifice (Heb. 11:4). Because he was righteous by faith, the sacrifice he made was acceptable to God — not to merit the forgiveness of sins and grace through this work, but to exercise his faith and display it to others, inviting them to believe. (Tappert: 134, Ap.IV [202])

III. Levitical Sacrifices and the One Propitiatory Sacrifice

It is of course necessary to deal with the meaning of sacrifice in the Old Testament. Thus, Chemnitz includes a brief interpretive description of the Levitical sacrifices early in his treatment of the sacrificial Mass. The *true* and *real* sacrifices, he concludes, are *not* the animals and ceremonial offerings of the Old Testament, but rather the Sacrifice of Christ and the spiritual or eucharistic sacrifices of believers. Contrariwise, it is common to find references to the "figurative" or "metaphorical" sacrifices of the New Testament, as though these were the shadows instead of the substance. But the shadowy metaphors are actually found in the Levitical sacrifices, for which reason the Apology states: "As we discern the shadow in the Old Testament, so in the New we should look for [the real sacrifice] it represents and not for another symbol that seems to be a sacrifice" (Tappert: 257, Ap.XXIV [36]). Which is to say that neither the Mass *ex opere operato,* nor the mere outward performance of sacrifices in the Old Testament, is the *true* Christian sacrifice.[13]

13 In his *Commentary on Romans,* Melanchthon writes:

Melanchthon does describe the Old Testament sacrifices as either propitiatory or eucharistic, as defined above. However, those that are called propitiatory, or sin–sacrifices, did not merit the forgiveness of sins. Instead, they signified the Sacrifice of Christ and thereby held the Gospel out to the people of God. At the same time, they also earned "forgiveness" in the sense of civil righteousness. For within the theocracy of Israel, those who sinned against the community were allowed to remain by the offering of a required sacrifice.[14] "One might obtain a certain forgiveness of sins through such a sacrifice, in that a person so reconciled might not be excluded from the synagogue or the Jewish commu-

> In the Old Testament slaughters of cattle and other ceremonies were performed which at that time had a command of God and foreshadowed the benefits of the Gospel. These shadows ceased after the Gospel was revealed. Since the New Testament brings righteousness and life in the hearts, worship and sacrifices should now be true and constant impulses of the heart, a constant glorification of God, as Christ says [Jn 4:24]: "The true worshipers will worship God in spirit and in truth," that is, with true and spiritual impulses of the heart. That is what Paul wants here [Romans 12:1] when he calls for a rational worship, that is, worship of the mind, in which God is acknowledged and apprehended, in which there are true impulses toward God — fear, faith, calling on God, and confession. Paul rules out no only animal sacrifices, but also the works of men, and not only the traditions of the monks, but also moral works whenever they are done without fear of God and without faith. The saying of Paul fights everywhere with the opinion of the *opus operatum*. (Romans: 211)

14 "Certain of these [Levitical sacrifices] are mentioned in the law as propitiatory sacrifices because of their significance or similarity, not because they merited the remission of sins before God, but because they signified or were a sign of the sacrifice of Christ which was to come. But there they merited the remission of sins in outward life, that is, so that they were not excluded from the Mosaic civil life. Thus they were called propitiatory sacrifices for sin [sin offerings] or sacrifices for transgressions." LC43: 151. Cf. also Tappert: 252, Ap.XXIV (21)

nity" (LC55: 223–224). In this way, in keeping with their primary function of pointing towards Christ, the Levitical sacrifices identified the Children of Israel, from whom the Savior would come.

Regardless of what the Old Testament sacrifices were called,"there has really been only one propitiatory sacrifice in the world, the death of Christ, as the Epistle to the Hebrews teaches (10:4), 'It is impossible that the blood of bulls and goats should take away sins'" (Tappert: 253, Ap.XXIV [22]). Just as the Lutherans confess in AC XXIV:

> Scripture shows in many places that there is no sacrifice for original sin, or for any other sin, except the one death of Christ. For it is written in the Epistle to the Hebrews that Christ offered himself once and by this offering made satisfaction for all sin. It is an unprecedented novelty in church doctrine that Christ's death should have made satisfaction only for original sin and not for other sins as well. (Tappert: 58–59, AC XXIV [26])[15]

By virtue of this once–for–all Sacrifice, Christ brought an end to the ceremonial sacrifices of the Old Testament. "After

---

15 Melanchthon also writes in his *Loci Communes*:

It is a very important matter to offer a sacrifice. To sacrifice is to acknowledge the wrath of God against the sins of the human race, to subject oneself to this wrath, to be the mediator between God and the human race, and to enter into the holy of holies with God. Therefore it is said in Heb. 9[:12], "Through His own blood He entered once into the holy of holies, having obtained eternal redemption." Again [v. 14], "who through the eternal Spirit offered Himself without spot to God." Christ offered Himself. We are to acknowledge that this sacrifice was made by Him, and believe that through it the eternal Father has been reconciled to us, and we should give thanks for it. Godly people should consider these things and seek out the true testimonies of the ancient church. (LC43: 150)

the revelation of the Gospel they had to stop" (Tappert: 253, Ap.XXIV [22]).[16]

IV. Eucharistic Sacrifices and the Worship of the Heart

Because the one, eternally–significant, propitiatory sacrifice of Christ on the Cross brought an end to the "propitiatory sacrifices" of the Old Testament, in the New Testament there remains no other sacrifice than the sacrifice of praise (the *eucharistic* sacrifice). To make *this* sacrifice, "we should flee for refuge not to our own works but to grace and mercy." In doing so, "the confession of sin and thirst for grace will be the voice of the new people. . . . These are the proper bulls; that is, thanksgiving and the preaching of the Gospel. This is what the sacrifices of the Old Testament signify" (LW 18:74 [1524]).

With these words, Luther not only maintains the existence of a New Testament sacrifice; he paints in broad strokes the nature of that sacrifice. It is the "sacrifice of praise" and of "thanksgiving." It includes fleeing from our own works in order to find refuge in the grace and mercy of God. It is the "confession of sin" and the "thirst for grace." It requires the "preaching of the Gospel." In all of these actions of praise, however, there can be no propitiatory sacrifice in

16 "Certainly there is no more than one sacrifice which takes away sin, for the sin–sacrifices in the law were so called only for the sake of what the signify, the one sacrifice on the cross, *Christ.* Therefore, since *Christ* is revealed, since he has come, they are abolished, for they were only the shadows of the true reconciliation, as St. Paul declares, 'Therefore, since the truth, Christ, is revealed, they have ceased' [Cf. Heb 10:1,9–14]." (LC55: 224). Lest there be any doubt, the destruction of Jerusalem — and of the Temple, in particular — in a.d. 70, as prophecied by Christ in the Gospels, brought a divine halt to the sacrificial cult.

addition to the Sacrifice of Christ. Rather, on the basis of His Cross, His people offer up the eucharistic sacrifice.

Clearly, this eucharistic sacrifice is not restricted to the Lord's Supper; rather, it defines the entire new life of believers in Christ. It is the sacrificial worship of the heart, brought by those who have already been reconciled to God by the Crucifixion of His Son. As such, it can only be offered by faith, and faith itself is the beginning of the eucharistic sacrifice. Thus, Melanchthon defines the "sacrifice of praise" as "the proclamation of the Gospel, faith, prayer, thanksgiving, confession, the affliction of the saints, yes, all the good works of the saints" (Tappert: 253, Ap.XXIV [25]).[17] Understood in this comprehensive sense, the eucharistic sacrifice must be viewed, not as a means to an end, but as *the end* in itself. The eucharistic sacrifice, that is, the worship of God in all its various aspects, "is in fact *the* ultimate purpose of the church, and must give meaning, direction, and impetus to all particular functions and activities of the church, including the great missionary task."[18]

We begin to see just how broad the definition of eucharistic sacrifice can be. But this broadness should not be surprising. Priesthood and sacrifice belong together, and just as the New Testament brought an end to the Levitical priesthood and highlighted the *priesthood* of all believers in

---

17 Melanchthon repeats himself *verbatim* in the *Loci Communes* of 1543: "In our era eucharistic sacrifices still remain. They are called sacrifices of praise, the preaching of the Gospel, faith, invocation, the giving of thanks, confession, the afflictions of the saints, indeed all the good works of the saints" (LC43: 151).

18 Kurt E. Marquart, "Liturgical Commonplaces," *Concordia Theological Quarterly* 42 (October 1978): 340

Christ, so too were the Old Testament sacrifices displaced by the whole spectrum of activities performed in faith by believers. Luther's fondness for the royal priesthood therefore included an appreciation for the eucharistic sacrifice. Notwithstanding his polemics against the Roman Mass, on account of which he often avoids the term *sacrifice*, Luther certainly does not regard the eucharistic sacrifice itself an optional matter. As Chemnitz puts it: "All Christians are priests — not that all should function without difference in the ministry of the Word and of the Sacraments, without a special call, but that they should offer spiritual sacrifices."[19] Which is to say, in the words of Melanchthon: "All of us are priests. The priesthood is nothing more than the right to pray, or to importune God, or to make an offering to God."[20] Another consequence of neglecting the eucharistic sacrifice has therefore been the common misinterpretation, according to which the royal priesthood is viewed as the "pastorhood of all believers." Of course, this misunderstanding has also failed to grasp the insight, that the New Testament does not refer to the Apostolic Ministry of Word and Sacrament as

---

19 Chemnitz, *Ministry, Word, and Sacraments: An Enchiridion (MWS)*, tr. Luther Poellot (St. Louis, 1981): 29

20 Melanchthon, *Propositions on the Mass*, tr. Charles Hill, in *Melanchthon: Selected Writings*, ed. Flack and Satre (Minneapolis, 1962): 67. Or, as he explains at greater length in his *Commentary on Romans*: "Priests properly have three duties: to hold fast and to confess the Gospel, which has been divinely revealed; to have a command and promise about invocation; and sacrifice. These belong first to Christ, through whom the Gospel has been revealed, who alone has the right of interceding for us, and of offering his sacrifices for others. Thereafter, Christ imparts the honor of the priesthood to the believers, because he gives them his Word, adds the promise that God will hear those who call on him, and gives them the fruit of his sacrifice. Then he demands sacrifices from them themselves, namely, confession and obedience in good works and afflictions." (*Romans*: 210)

a "priesthood." The priesthood is rather one of eucharistic sacrifice; of faith, prayer, and thanksgiving.[21]

Three New Testament passages in particular refer to this eucharistic sacrifice: 1 Peter 2:5, Romans 12:1, and Hebrews 13:15. Melanchthon comments on each of these in the Apology. With respect to the Petrine passage, for example, "Spiritual sacrifices are contrasted not only with the sacrifices of cattle but also with human works offered *ex opere operato*, for 'spiritual' refers to the operation of the Holy Spirit within us" (Tappert: 253, Ap.XXIV [25]).

Especially important is a facet that always remains at the heart of the spiritual sacrifice, namely, the sacrificial slaying of the Old Adam. "Just as faith is something more than psychic reception of facts, sacrifice is more than devo-

---

21 Ottfried Koch writes: "The sacrifice of believers is the exercise of the universal priesthood. This doctrine is obscured these days by the notion that the ministry and the universal priesthood are in competition — a situation which has come about because the ministry has separated its function from that of the universal priesthood in a manner foreign to the New Testament." As Koch explains, the function of the ministry is the bestowal of Christ's gifts in the Gospel and Sacraments; the function of the universal priesthood is the faithful reception of those gifts. Thus, the ministry and the priesthood belong always together in a complementary relationship. "The separation of the ministry from the universal priesthood is harmful to both, since neither the special function of the ministry nor the special function of the Christian estate as priesthood is taken into account. The counterpart of the universal priesthood is the priesthood of the whole people of Israel. And just as the Israelitic priesthood did, the universal priesthood belongs *within* the context of the covenant — in this case, the New Covenant. It is a priesthood established *on the basis of* the atonement and presupposes it as its source of life." Ottfried Koch, *Presence or Re–Presentation* (an unpublished English translation of the German, *Gegenwart oder Vergegenwärtigung*, Munich: Claudius Verlag, 1965), tr. Oliver K. Olson: 171–172.

tion in the realm of sentiment. The sacrifice of the faithful is a receptive dying of the old and a resurrection of the new Adam" (Koch: 173). The eucharistic sacrifice, therefore, does not consist in giving up some portion of one's property, but rather in the total surrender of one's life to the will and purposes of God. Yet, because He is gracious and loving, surrendering to the will of God means trusting His mercy and relying on Him alone for everything. In short, the sacrifice is *faith*. Thus, the "spiritual worship" of Romans 12:1 "is a worship in which the spirit knows and takes hold of God, as it does when it fears and trusts him" (Tappert: 253, Ap.XXIV [25]).

Like Melanchthon, Luther also emphasizes self–surrender and mortification. "It belongs properly to all who live under the cross," he writes, "to slay and kill themselves and the lusts and desires of the Adam in them, so that this sacrifice of praise will be as the smoke and fragrance of the sacrifices of the law" (LW 36:145–146 [1521]). Here, by referring to those "who live under the cross," Luther indicates that the eucharistic sacrifice is always made solely on the basis of the propitiatory Sacrifice offered once for all by Christ. Anything offered to God apart from such faith in Christ is no longer eucharistic. Indeed, the numerous definitions given to the eucharistic sacrifice would be confusing, if it were not understood that essentially the sacrifice is always faith. All else flows from this faith, and is acceptable to God only because of faith, which first of all lays hold of Christ and His forgiveness. As Melanchthon writes in the Apology, on the basis of the passage from Hebrews (13:15): "He commands them to offer praises, that is, prayer, thanksgiving, confession, and the like. These are valid, not *ex opere operato* but because of faith. We see this from the phrase, 'Through him let us offer,' namely, through faith in Christ" (Tappert: 253, Ap.XXIV [25]).

Essentially, the sacrifice of mortification and the sacrifice of faith are simply two sides of the same coin. For as the Old Adam is destroyed, faith looks to Christ alone for all things; faith sees nothing whatsoever but Christ and His merits, and so also confesses what He has done. Such confession is the purest form of praise and thanksgiving to God. This eucharistic sacrifice, which acknowledges no one but Christ, should be on the lips of Christians at all times.

True Christian Worship is *Spiritual*

The Lutheran Reformers typically cite the Word of Jesus, that "those who worship God must worship in spirit and truth" (St. John 4:24), as a clear condemnation of "the notion that the sacrifices are valid *ex opere operato*." Quite to the contrary, "it teaches that worship should be in spirit, in faith, and with the heart." Or, to put it very simply: "The worship of the New Testament is spiritual; it is the righteousness of faith in the heart and the fruits of faith" (Tappert: 254, Ap.XXIV [27]).[22]

---

22 Melanchthon says much the same thing in his *Loci* of 1555:

In the New Testament worship is not just external forms and showy works, but is a divine light, faith, fear, comfort, and joy in God in the heart; and the beginning of eternal life and suitable works follow the divine light and life in the heart, as the prophet says, "I will put my law within them, and I will write it upon their hearts" [Jer. 31:33]. And Christ says in John 4:23, "The true worshipers will worship the Father in spirit and in truth." Therefore, the ceremonies and sacrifices of the law of Moses are abolished, for the New Testament demands spiritual sacrifices of the heart, that is, true faith, true fear of God, and from this the external fruit of faith. (LC55: 225–226)

And yet, as simple as this definition seems, "*faith*" itself can be so commonly misunderstood.[23] Among both the Protestant and the Roman churches alike, many would argue that justifying faith must be *formed* by love and *activated* by works; that faith must be "put into action." No doubt, there is some truth to this. God does command love for the neighbor, and good works always follow faith. What is more, genuine love for the neighbor and the good works of faith are indeed a pleasing eucharistic sacrifice. However, these sacrifices must always be understood from the proper perspective. *Loving your neighbor as yourself*, for example, is always contingent on *loving God with all your heart, with all your soul, and with all your mind* (St. Luke 10:26–28).[24] And

In his treatise on *The Adoration of the Sacrament*, Luther explains such true "spiritual worship" according to the precise meaning of the term *worship*, only now applied to the activity of the believing heart:

> It is the adoration or bowing of the heart, so that from the bottom of your heart you thereby show and confess yourself to be his subordinate creature. For from this you see that true worship can be nothing else than faith; it is faith's sublimest activity with respect to God. For no one is capable of such heartfelt confession, adoration, bending, and bowing (or whatever else you want to call it) before God in his heart, unless he unwaveringly holds God to be his Lord and Father, from whom he receives and will receive all good things, and through whom, without any merit on his part, he is redeemed and preserved from all sins and evil. (LW 36:292–293 [1523])

23 *Cf., e.g.*, Melanchthon's extended discussion of "faith" in the Introduction to his *Commentary on Romans*: 28ff.

24 Melanchthon comments in his lectures on *Paul's Letter to the Colossians* (1:3–8):

> The saints do good because they know that this is what God wants, and because they value his will above the promised rewards. Their action is not prompted by the desire to earn something in return. For they know that all things have already been given freely, and that they cannot be won by any human merits, nor given their due value by them. On the contrary, these same rewards stir them up and set them on fire, so that they long to please

such love for God is above all else a godly fear and trust in Him.[25] Thus, putting "faith into action" is not primarily a matter of what we do for others, but the exercise of faith itself, that is, opening up the "hand" of faith to *receive* everything from God.[26] As Lutherans confess: "Faith is that worship which receives God's offered blessings; the righteousness of the law is that worship which offers God our own merits. It is by faith that God wants to be worshiped, namely, that we receive from him what he promises and offers" (Tappert: 114, Ap.IV [49]). Obeying the First Commandment, from which all the others flow, does not consist in doing something for God, but rather in trusting God to do all things for us in and through Christ. In this way, everything is turned around to be exactly the opposite of the *opinio legis*. So also

> God in their turn, and to show all the gratitude they can. Nor are these good actions the price with which the reward is bought. They are signs of gratitude for the reward already received and possessed. (*Colossians*: 34)

25 In a discussion of the woman who anointed Jesus' feet (St. Luke 7:36–50), Melanchthon writes in the Apology:

> The account here shows what he calls "love." The woman came, believing that she should seek the forgiveness of sins from Christ. This is the highest way of worshiping Christ. Nothing greater could she ascribe to him. By looking for the forgiveness of sins from him, she truly acknowledged him as the Messiah. Truly to believe means to think of Christ in this way, and in this way to worship and take hold of him. . . . He points to the woman and praises her reverence, her anointing and crying, all of which were a sign and confession of faith that she was looking for the forgiveness of sins from Christ. (Tappert: 128, Ap.IV [154])

26 "*Fiducia* is an act of the will; it has to do with man's inner life, his heart, and it is present 'when my heart, and the Holy Ghost in the heart, says: The promise of God is true and certain. Of this faith Scripture speaks' [Ap. IV (113)]. To have faith in the Christian and Biblical sense means much more than merely holding certain ideas about God. It means to say yes to God's promise, to be willing to accept what God has promised man, to trust in the promise of God's mercy — a trust in God without reservation. One cannot speak of faith in this sense apart from the Word of promise." (Fagerberg:156)

with our sacrifice. We do not sacrifice in order to offer God some manner of payment; we sacrifice ourselves in order to let God be God for us.[27] Which means fixing our eyes on Christ alone by faith. And if we understand that faith in Christ means setting aside absolutely everything else, beginning with our own selves, then the concept of *sacrifice* becomes clear.[28] By the same token, any theology or faith that does not have Christ, not only as its most important but as its *only* object, has failed to offer the eucharistic sacrifice. Setting *anything* alongside Christ establishes the equivalent of another sacrificial Mass.

Now, let us be clear: Even though the eucharistic sacrifice is sometimes called the sacrifice of the *New Testament,* in contrast to the outward sacrifices of the Old Testament, it should not be thought that this true sacrifice and worship of the heart was something new with the Incarnation. From the start, faith in Christ alone has been necessary for the proper service of God. As Melanchthon makes clear:

27 "The sacrificial action of the universal priesthood is a receptive action. Following the premise that Christ's sacrifice must be interpreted on the basis of the doctrine of atonement, it is clear that the sacrifice of believers must be understood as *faith,* which receives the atonement. Faith and sacrifice are identical in content. In similar ways they imply man's surrender to God." (Koch: 173)

28 "If now we consider that we are sacrifices, we shall understand that we have been called, not to pleasure, riches, and power of this world, but to a violent death, dreadful hatred, and afflictions of every kind as we are attacked by the devil and by wicked men. And even as the sacrificial animal stands by the altar, constantly waiting until it is struck down, so let us stand at the altar, that is, in confession and glorification of God. Let us render obedience to God in persecutions and calamities as we are besieged. In the midst of them let us call on God and believe that these acts of worship are pleasing because of Christ, for whose sake we shall also be set free at some time." (*Romans*: 212)

> The Old Testament prophets also condemn the popular notion of worship *ex opere operato* and teach spiritual righteousness and sacrifice. Jer. 7:22, 23,"I did not speak to your fathers or command them concerning burnt offerings and sacrifices. But this command I gave them, 'Obey my voice, and I will be your God.'" Clearly God had commanded the fathers concerning burnt offerings and sacrifices, but what Jeremiah is condemning is an idea of sacrifices that did not come from God, namely, that such worship pleased him *ex opere operato*. He adds that God had commanded faith. (Tappert: 254, Ap.XXIV [27])[29]

In Ap.IV, Melanchthon understands this hypocrisy of reliance on sacrifice *ex opere operato* as being similar to the Roman Catholic doctrine of works. In each case, the role of faith is ignored. Thus the papacy should heed the warning, that not works but faith alone is the true worship of God:

> It is strange that our opponents make so little of faith

29 Melanchthon had also commented in Ap.IV on such abuses of the Old Testament sacrifice:

> The Gentiles had sacrifices which they took over from the patriarchs. They imitated their works but did not keep their faith, believing that these works were a propitiation and price that reconciled God to them. The people of the Old Testament imitated these sacrifices with the notion that on account of them they had a gracious God, so to say, *ex opere operato*. Here we see how vehemently the prophets rebuke the people. Ps. 50:8,"I do not reprove you for your sacrifices." And Jer. 7:22,"I did not command concerning burnt offerings." Such passages do not condemn the sacrifices that God surely commanded as outward observances in the state, but they do condemn the wicked belief of those who did away with faith in the notion that through these works they placated the wrath of God. Because no works can put the conscience at rest, they kept thinking up new works beyond God's commandment. (Tappert: 135, Ap.IV [206])

> when they see it praised everywhere as the foremost kind of worship, as in Ps. 50:15: "Call upon me in the day of trouble; I will deliver you, and you shall glorify me." This is how God wants to be known and worshiped, that we accept his blessings and receive them because of his mercy rather than because of our own merits. (Tappert: 115, Ap.IV [59])

This true spiritual worshiping and honoring of God by faith has always included two different aspects:—one, that we first recognize our dire trouble and need apart from Christ our Savior, and two, that we then call upon Him for help.[30] As such, "worship" properly consists of repentance in the broad sense: contrition and faith. Apart from faith, which looks to Christ for help, God's judgment against sin leads only to despair. This factor was the critical difference between Peter and Judas, for example; Peter had faith and was uplifted, but Judas did not and so ended his life in deep despair. When Jesus invites the sinner, "Come to Me, all who labor and are heavy laden, and I will give you rest" (St. Matthew 11:28), He is urging faith in His forgiveness. Coming to Christ is equivalent to believing in Him. The same thing is expressed even more clearly in St. Mark 1:15, "Repent, and believe in the Gospel." Both the contrition and the faith are the work of God, the work of His Law and of His Gospel. In contrition, God demolishes the sinner; in faith, He brings the humbled one to life. "The Lord kills and brings to life; He brings down to Sheol and raises up" (1 Samuel 2:6). But of

---

30 "Ps. 50:13, 15 also condemns the idea of sacrifices *ex opere operato*. It rejects sacrificial victims and requires prayer: 'Do I eat the flesh of bulls? Call upon me in the day of trouble; I will deliver you, and you shall glorify me.' It declares that calling upon God is really worshiping and honoring him." (Tappert: 255, Ap.XXIV [29])

these two works, the Gospel is God's *opus proprium*, whereby He comforts the broken–hearted and brings them to new life in Christ. Comprehended by this activity of God, the contrite believer offers up the eucharistic sacrifice, which is repentance and faith. (Cf. Tappert: 187–189, Ap.XII [44–50])

The bottom line of course is this, that simply going through the outward motions of *any* ceremony does not in itself make for a eucharistic sacrifice. To be sure, Lutherans do not object to the use of ceremony. In fact, ceremony is beneficial, but only as a means whereby the heart of faith renders its sacrifice of praise. The eucharistic sacrifice of *faith* is the determining factor. Where faith is present, the outward motions of "prayer, proclamation of the Gospel, confession," and the whole "ceremony of the Mass" become a eucharistic sacrifice "through which the name of the Lord becomes great." Together, these various ceremonies of the true believers indicate outwardly the continuous or "daily" sacrifice of the Church, which Melanchthon describes on the basis of Numbers 28.

> Num. 28:4*ff*. list three parts of this daily sacrifice, the burning of the lamb, the drink offering, and the offering of flour. The Old Testament had pictures or shadows of what was to come; thus this depicted Christ and the whole worship of the New Testament. The burning of the lamb symbolizes the death of Christ. The drink offering symbolizes the sprinkling, that is, the sanctifying of believers throughout the world with the blood of that lamb, by the proclamation of the Gospel, as Peter says: "Sanctified by the Spirit for obedience to Jesus Christ and for sprinkling with his blood." The offering of flour

> symbolizes faith, prayer, and thanksgiving in the heart. (Tappert, 257, Ap.XXIV [36])[31]

Here again, the outward sacrifices of the Old Testament are described as the symbols or expressions of the true, eucharistic sacrifice of faith. For example, the Old Testament sacrifices are often said to signify in particular the mortification of the Old Adam. This aspect of the eucharistic sacrifice appears over and over again throughout Ap.XXIV. By way of example:

> The slaughter of animals in the Old Testament symbolized both the death of Christ and the proclamation of the Gospel, which should kill this old flesh and begin a new and eternal life in us. (Tappert: 256, Ap.XXIV [34])[32]

By its very nature, *sacrifice* involves a death, and whatever would be sacrificed must be killed. Thus, the new priesthood offers itself into death, and each Christian offers himself or herself. The victim is the priest, or more accurately,

---

31 Luther explains the "sprinkling" as follows: "The Sacraments, Baptism and the Lord's Supper, belong to this sprinkling, for in both we are sprinkled with the blood of Christ. In Baptism we are baptized into the death of Christ (Rom. 6:3), and in the Lord's Supper the body and blood of Christ are distributed to the church. In the ministry of the Word similarly we hear this sprinkling, that Christ has made satisfaction for the sins of the world. Here nothing remains but this: As we hear this in the Word and as it is offered and shown to us in the symbols of our faith, we should firmly believe, and we should strengthen our minds with trust in this sprinkling." (LW 12:363 [1532])

32 Or, again: "Since the priesthood of the New Testament is a ministry of the Spirit, as Paul teaches in II Cor. 3:6, the only sacrifice of satisfaction for the sins of others is the sacrifice of Christ. . . . It offers to others the Gospel and the sacraments so that thereby they may receive faith and the Holy Spirit and be put to death and made alive." (Tappert: 260, Ap.XXIV [59])

the *Old Adam* with all his wicked lusts and sinful desires. To make this sacrifice, the Christian submits to the preaching of God's Word, both Law and Gospel. Thus, the eucharistic sacrifice is understood to be the very essence and character of the Christian life, that is, a daily exercise of Baptism.[33]

Lutherans Do Retain the Daily Sacrifice

In contrast to their Roman opponents, who "imagine that [the daily sacrifice] symbolizes the ceremony alone," the Lutherans define the daily sacrifice (Malachi 1:11) as "preaching the Gospel, being put to death and being made alive" (Tappert: 257, Ap.XXIV [39]).[34] And since the Lutherans

---

33 Cf. Melanchthon's comments in his lectures on *Paul's Letter to the Colossians*: 60–62

34 Because the Roman Confutation had given so much attention to Malachi 1:11, ostensibly as proof for the sacrificial Mass, Melanchthon likewise addresses this Prophecy at some length. He interprets the passage as referring to the eucharistic sacrifice of the New Testament, as we have already defined; not to some new external sacrifice as the Roman Catholics had argued.

> The New Testament teaches that there should be a new and pure sacrifice; this is faith, prayer, thanksgiving, confession and proclamation of the Gospel, suffering because of the Gospel, etc. About such sacrifices Malachi says (1:11), "From the rising of the sun to its setting my name is great among the nations, and in every place incense is offered to my name, and a pure offering."... The name of the Lord will be great. This takes place through the proclamation of the Gospel, which makes known the name of Christ and the Father's mercy promised in Christ. The proclamation of the Gospel produces faith in those who accept it. They call upon God, they give thanks to God, they bear afflictions in confession, they do good works for the glory of Christ. This is how the name of the Lord becomes great among the nations. (Tappert: 255, Ap.XXIV [30,31])
>
> Luther likewise interprets:
>
> Incense we take as prayer. Word and prayer, therefore, are the two sacrifices of Christians. Prayer takes place along with thanksgiving and praise. The sacrifice of Christians is clean, because they themselves are without fault, because they have been washed by the blood of Christ, etc. Unbelievers

surely do maintain and emphasize "preaching the Gospel" and "being put to death and being made alive," as shown above, "good men can easily see the falsity of the charge that we do away with the daily sacrifice" (Tappert: 257, Ap.XXIV [41]). Actually, the Roman Catholics were the ones who had abolished the daily sacrifice, since they had buried the Gospel and allowed faith to fall by the wayside. By the sacrifice of the Mass, they had established a false sacrifice that actually destroyed the true eucharistic sacrifice. As Melanchthon points out in the Apology:

> If the use of the sacrament were the daily sacrifice, we could lay more claim to observing it than our opponents because in their churches mercenary priests use the sacrament. In our churches the use is more frequent and more devout. It is the people who use it, and this only when they have been instructed and examined. Thus, since we keep both the proclamation of the Gospel and the proper use of the sacraments, we still have the daily sacrifice. (Tappert: 258, Ap.XXIV [49])

According to the Lutherans, the *proper use* of the Means of Grace — indeed, the total work of the Church in the Ministry of Word and Sacrament — is the sacrifice and God-given worship of the New Testament. It is the priestly office, both of those who preach or administer, and of those who listen and receive, by which they sacrifice the Old Adam and are engrafted into Christ. Hearing the Word of God and participating in His Holy Sacraments are the means by which faith is both created and sustained, and by

---

> offer no sacrifice. Christians do not offer a worthless, blind, lame, or false sacrifice but a faithful and pleasing one. If their heart is faithful, then their sin is not counted against them. (LW 18:397 [1526])

which Christ Himself is received — for that is the primary activity of faith — to the praise of His glorious grace. That is why, in the Divine Service God is always the "*Prime Mover*." God is the One who creates faith, and He is the One who gives all things to faith. Faith as the eucharistic sacrifice does not create worship; it only *receives* what God offers and gives through His Means of Grace.[35]

> Thus the service and worship of the Gospel is to receive good things from God, while the worship of the law is to offer and present our goods to God. We cannot offer anything to God unless we have first been reconciled and reborn. The greatest possible comfort comes from this doctrine that the highest worship in the Gospel is the desire to receive forgiveness of sins, grace, and righteousness. (Tappert: 155, Ap.IV [310])

By receiving this gracious Divine Service in faith, the people of Christ confess before God, before each other, and before the world that the Lord is gracious and merciful. And this confession of the grace and mercy of God in Christ is the priestly garment of the Church, by which she is dressed in the merits of Christ. Accordingly, Melanchthon asserts in the Apology: "The real adornment of the churches is godly, practical, and clear teaching, the godly use of the sacraments, ardent prayer, and the like" (Tappert: 259, Ap.XXIV [50]).[36]

---

35 "The sacrifice proper to a Christian is exclusively that of praise and thanksgiving, that is to say, one which receives Christ's sacrifice in faith.... The congregation's sacrifice, the mortification of the old man, is an inseparable part of Christ's work, and is the final goal of his sacrifice. The atonement is meant to be accepted by men in faith." (Koch: 188)

36 Melanchthon is clearly building on the AC; for that which creates the Church and so also marks her existence is the Ministry of the Gospel–Word and Sacrament. "In order that we may obtain this faith, the ministry

So also, then, does Luther define the New Testament "holy day" according to this "adornment," that is, the eucharistic sacrifices of the Church at worship.[37] And along these same lines, he devotes a rather lengthy "foreword" to his sermon, *On the Sum of the Christian Life*, to a discussion of the importance God places on *listening* to His Word (cf. LW 51:260–265 [1532]). Thus, for Luther and Melanchthon both, being in Church — which is to say, hearing God's Word and receiving the Sacrament — is the highest service and worship of God.

---

of teaching the Gospel and administering the sacraments was instituted. . . ." Accordingly, "the church is the assembly of saints in which the Gospel is taught purely and the sacraments are administered rightly." (Tappert: 31 & 32, AC V [1] & AC VII [1])

37 *Cf., e.g.*, LW 1:249–250 [1536]. Or, again, as he describes the Sabbath in his sermon at Torgau Castle Church:

> By the grace of God we know how this commandment concerning the sabbath is to be understood. . . It means . . . in the first place, to do something on that day which is a holy work, which is owing only to God, namely, that above all other things one preaches God's Word purely and holily. . . . And likewise, that the others hear and learn God's Word and help to see to it that it is purely preached and kept. This is what it means rightly to observe the day of rest and to "consecrate" or "sanctify" the place or the church. . . . Secondly, it means that we receive the Word of God, which we have heard in our hearts and with which we have thus been sprinkled, in order that it may bring forth power and fruit in us, and that we may publicly confess it and intend to hold on to it through life and through death. Thirdly, it means that when we have heard God's Word we also lift up to God our common, united incense, that is, that we call upon him and pray to him together (which we know is certainly pleasing and acceptable to him, particularly in common assembly), and also praise and thank God together with joy for all his benefits, temporal and eternal, and all the wonderful works he does in his church. Thus everything that is done in such an assembly of the whole congregation or church is nothing but holy, godly business and work and is a holy sabbath, in order both that God may be rightly and holily served and all men be helped. (LW 51:342–343 [1544])

V. Eucharistic Sacrifice and the Ceremony of the Lord's Supper

The Lutheran Reformers are well aware of Patristic references to the Eucharist as a sacrifice. However, they interpret the early fathers — not in terms of grace *ex opere operato*, or propitiatory sacrifice for "the remission of sins, of guilt, and of punishment for those to whom it is transferred" — but rather in terms of thanksgiving and the eucharistic sacrifice. "Hence [the fathers] call it 'eucharist'" (Tappert: 261, Ap.XXIV [66]).[38] As Melanchthon explains further:

38 Chemnitz writes in his Examination of Trent:

> The Lord's Supper is called Eucharist by the most ancient fathers, Ignatius, Justin, Irenaeus, *etc.* They do this, as Chrysostom explains, Homily 16, on Matthew, because in its celebration there is placed before us the contemplation of many and varied blessings of God, chiefly, however, of the foremost work of God's love toward us, that He sent His Son, who be delivering up His body and shedding His blood redeemed us lost ones, that in this way we might be challenged to thanksgiving. The sacrifice of praise and thanksgiving is frequently lauded in Scripture. The fathers apply the term "sacrifice" also to hymns, praises, and giving of thanks. (Chemnitz, Ex: 485)

Chemnitz then goes on to describe in greater detail a number of ways in which the early church fathers appropriately understood the Lord's Supper as a eucharistic sacrifice. *First*, the celebration of the Lord's Supper is considered a eucharistic sacrifice on account of the public preaching and solemn proclamation of the passion, death, resurrection, and ascension of Christ. *Second*, the celebration of the Lord's Supper is considered a eucharistic sacrifice because many exercises of true piety come together in the use of the Sacrament. *Third*, the celebration of the Lord's Supper is considered a eucharistic sacrifice because the whole Church together and the individual communicants solemnly vow, consecrate, and dedicate themselves wholly with body and soul to the Lord and, on account of the Lord, to their neighbor. (*cf.* Chemnitz, Ex: 485–486)

There are also some ways, Chemnitz indicates, in which the early church fathers understood the Sacrament itself to be a type of eucharistic sacrifice. First, the Sacrament of the Lord's Supper is considered a eucharistic sacrifice in the sense that it is a sacred action, or the administration of a sacred action.

> The Fathers speak of a twofold effect, of the comfort for the conscience and of thanksgiving or praise; the first of these belongs to the nature of the sacrament, and the second to the sacrifice. Ambrose says about the comfort: "Go to him and be absolved, for he is the forgiveness of sins. Do you ask who he is? Hear his own words (John 6:35), 'I am the bread of life; he who comes to me shall not hunger, and he who believes in me shall never thirst.'" This proves that the sacrament offers the forgiveness of sins and that it ought to be received by faith.
>
> There are also statements about thanksgiving, like the beautiful statement of Cyprian about the godly communicant, "Piety distinguishes between what is given and what is forgiven, and it gives thanks to the Giver of such a generous blessing." That is, piety looks at what is given and at what is forgiven; it compares the greatness of God's blessings with the greatness of our ills, our sin and our death; and it gives thanks. From this term "eucharist" arose in the church. (Tappert: 263, Ap.XXIV [75,76])

Melanchthon continues by applying Patristic references to "offering" to the entire act of worship:

> Even though the Mass is called an offering, what does that term have to do with these dreams about the efficacy of the act *ex opere operato* and its supposed applicability to

---

Second, the Sacrament of the Lord's Supper is considered a eucharistic sacrifice in the sense that it is a solemn memorial of the one Sacrifice of Christ. Third, and finally, the Sacrament of the Lord's Supper is considered a eucharistic sacrifice in the sense that the actual Sacrifice of the Cross — that is, not the sacrificial act, but the sacrificial Victim, the crucified Body and shed Blood of Christ — is present, dispensed, offered, and taken in the Lord's Supper. (*cf.* Chemnitz, Ex: 487–492)

> merit the forgiveness of sins for others? It can be called an offering, as it is called a eucharist, because prayers, thanksgivings, and the whole worship are offered there. But neither ceremonies nor prayers provide an advantage *ex opere operato* without faith. (Tappert: 265, Ap.XXIV [87])[39]

Melanchthon then cites a specific example:

> The Greek canon also says much about an offering; but it clearly shows that it is not talking about the body and blood of the Lord in particular, but about the whole service, about the prayers and thanksgivings. This is what it says: "And make us worthy to come to offer Thee entreaties and supplications and bloodless sacrifices for all the people." Properly understood, this is not offensive. It prays that we might be made worthy to offer prayers and supplications and bloodless sacrifices for the people. It calls even prayers "bloodless sacrifices." So it says a little later: "We offer Thee this reasonable and bloodless service." It is a misinterpretation to translate this as "reasonable victim" and apply it to the body of Christ itself. For the canon is talking about the whole service; and by "reasonable service" (Rom. 12:1) Paul meant the service of the mind, fear, faith, prayer, thanksgiving, and the like, in opposition to a theory of ex opere operato. (Tappert: 265, Ap.XXIV [88])

---

39 Or, as Melanchthon puts it in his *Loci Communes*:

Although the old scholars often use the word "sacrifice," they do not mean that priests sacrifice the Son of God, and that this work of the priests merits forgiveness of sins for others. As any rational person can easily determine, what they call sacrifice includes all that prayer, faith, participation, and giving thanks include. One ancient custom was to bring to the gathered company much bread and wine for the welfare of the poor; this was also called a sacrifice. (LC55: 222)

It is somewhat remarkable and certainly noteworthy that Melanchthon so easily reconciles this Greek Anaphora (or Eucharistic Prayer) with the Lutheran understanding of Scripture. Whether or not the Greeks who were using this prayer understood it precisely in this way is perhaps another matter. But Melanchthon's interpretation demonstrates the possibility of using sacrificial language in a wholesome and Scriptural manner. And the prayer that God would "make us worthy" is clearly of the essence of a eucharistic sacrifice. It acknowledges our own unworthiness and the need for God's mercy and forgiveness as we come before Him with our "prayers and supplications."

The Eucharist Is a Central Part of the Daily Sacrifice

In keeping with their understanding of the church fathers, the Lutherans are gladly willing to "include the ceremony [of the Mass]" among the eucharistic sacrifices of the Church, so long as this terminology is not taken "to mean that by itself, or *ex opere operato,* the ceremony is beneficial" (Tappert: 255, Ap.XXIV [33]). The most important thing at this point is the need to distinguish between the Sacrament itself and the ceremony in which it is received. These are logically two separate matters, even though they should never be separated in practice. The Lord's Supper, in and of itself, is purely God's gift to His people and is therefore not a sacrifice. The proper use of the Sacrament, however, including the faith that receives God's gift and the whole liturgical context of the ceremony, does rightly belong to the category of eucharistic sacrifice. The main question then must be, *in what sense* is the ceremony of the Mass a sacrifice?

As Luther quips in one of his "table talks":

> At the diet [of Augsburg] the papists tried to frighten and threaten us. They wished us to agree that the mass is a sacrifice of praise merely to provide themselves with a subterfuge in the term "sacrifice." I'm ready to concede to them that the mass is a sacrifice of praise, provided they on their part concede that it's not only the priest at the altar but every communicant who "sacrifices." (LW 54:139 [1532], *No.* 1325)

Chemnitz is far more detailed and precis. In his *Examination*, he enumerates no less than seven different ways in which the Lutherans rightly do regard the liturgy of the Eucharist as a sacrifice:

> 1. Because in the Communion service the prophetic and apostolic writings are read, the death of Christ is announced there, and the causes and benefits of the suffering Christ are set forth for consideration from the Word of God, the Mass could for this reason be called a sacrifice according to Scripture (Rom. 15:16; Phil. 2:17; and 1 Peter 2:5–9)....
>
> 2. In the adminstration of the Lord's Supper the praises of God are repeated, told, and sung. Now the sacrifice of praise has the testimony of Scripture (Heb. 13:15; Ps. 50:14–15)....
>
> 3. On account of public prayers and common thanksgivings the term "sacrifice" could, according to the meaning of Scripture, be given to the Mass....
>
> 4. Because a contribution of alms for the poor was al-

ways customary at the celebration of the Lord's Supper, the term "sacrifice" could for this reason, according to Scripture, be applied to the total action....

5. In the Communion service the whole man consecrates himself to God, and this is done in order that we may by this holy union inhere in God. Here, in the true use of the Lord's Supper, there is an exercise of repentance and faith; here love of God and of the neighbor is kindled. If anyone would call the Mass a sacrifice for this reason, and would apply the things themselves rightly, he would be doing nothing foreign to Scripture....

6. Because the blessing or consecration of the Eucharist is an act of the Gospel ministry, it could to this extent and with the addition of this declaration admit and bear the name "sacrifice," as Paul (Rom. 15:16) calls the total ministry of the Gospel a sacrifice....

7. Because the dispensation and participation or Communion of the Eucharist is done in commemoration of the one and only sacrifice of Christ, and because the sacrificial victim, who was once offered on the cross for our sins, is dispensed and taken there, it could for this reason, and with this explanation added, be called a sacrifice, even though Scripture does not so call it. (Chemnitz, Ex: 444–445)[40]

---

40 While the discussion of Chemnitz in his Examination of Trent is far and away the most exhaustive Lutheran treatment of sacrifice in the Eucharist, other Lutheran dogmaticians have also used the term and concept of sacrifice in connection with the Lord's Supper. By way of example, Hollazius writes (as cited by Charles Evanson in "Worship and Sacrifice," CTQ 42 [1978]):

> The word sacrifice may be used either literally or figuratively. Figuratively, it is used (1.) for every act which is done that we may cleave to God in holy fellowship, having in view the end that we may be truly happy. (2.) For the worship in the New Testament and the preaching of the Gospel (Rom.

And Melanchthon, in the Apology, is quite succinct and to the point in his assessment:

> Among the praises of God or sacrifices of praise we include the proclamation of the Word. In the same way, the reception of the Lord's Supper itself can be praise or thanksgiving, but it does not justify *ex opere operato* or merit the forgiveness of sins when it is transferred to others. (Tappert: 255, Ap.XXIV [33])[41]

It must be emphasized once again, that the sacrifice is never found in the outward action of the Sacrament alone, nor indeed in any outward ceremony *ex opere operato*. Rather, the whole liturgical context of the Eucharist is offered as a spiritual sacrifice *when it is offered in spirit and truth*, that is to

---

15:16; Phil. 2:17). (3.) For kindness and the works of charity toward our neighbour (Phil. 4:8; Heb. 13:16). (4.) For prayers and giving of thanks to God (Heb. 13:15; Rev. 5:8). . . . We do not deny that the Mass, or the celebration of the Eucharist may be figuratively called a sacrifice, because (1.) it is a work which is done that we may cleave to God in holy fellowship. (2.) It is not the least part of the worship of the New Testament. (3.) Formerly, when the Eucharist was celebrated, gifts were usually offered which fell to the use of the ministers of the Church and of the poor. (4.) The administration of the Holy Supper was joined with prayers and the giving of thanks. (5.) It was instituted in memory of the sacrifice of Christ . . . offered upon the altar of the cross. (Evanson: 367)

41 Luther is willing to agree on this same point:

We are ready to concede and to permit not the sacrament itself but the reception or use of the sacrament, to be called a sacrifice, with this difference and understanding: First, that it is not called an interpretative sacrifice or sacrifice of works but a sacrifice of thanksgiving; this means that whoever receives the sacrament is supposed to do it as a sign of thanksgiving by which he shows that he, as far as his own person is concerned, is thankful in his heart to Christ for his suffering and grace.

(LW 38:120–121 [1530])

say, when it is offered by faith. Whatever part of the worship service is embraced by faith — including the celebration of the Lord's Supper — thereby becomes a eucharistic sacrifice.[42] On this basis, Melanchthon can write rather pointedly in the Apology:

> We are perfectly willing for the Mass to be understood as a daily sacrifice, provided this means the whole Mass, the ceremony and also the proclamation of the Gospel, faith, prayer, and thanksgiving. Taken together, these are the daily sacrifice of the New Testament; the ceremony [of the Mass] was instituted because of them and ought not be separated from them. (Tappert: 256, Ap. XXIV [35])[43]

---

42 "The most intense form of sacrifice understood in this way is the hearing of the word of reconciliation and the reception of Christ's body and blood. Other elements which are commonly designated as sacrifice can properly be so-called only if they remain in the context of this believing reception. It is legitimate to call worship a sacrifice of praise and thanksgiving since, and insofar as, the praise is receptive of God's gifts. It may be called a sacrifice of prayer since, and insofar as, the one praying praises the giver and not himself in his prayer. It may be called a sacrifice of love since, and insofar as, the one reconciled is prepared for the work of reconciling love." (Koch: 174)

43 In his 1543 *Loci*, Melanchthon names three reasons for the ceremonies of the Lord's Supper:

> First, they are a personal admonition to those using them of the promise and of God's will toward us. Through them faith toward God is aroused in us and strengthened.
>
> The second reason was and is that the memory of the event may be publicly more lasting and the promise more faithfully passed on to all posterity. . . .
>
> The third reason was and is that the rites may be the basis for the public gathering together. For God wills that there be the public ministry of the Gospel. . . . He wants it to be heard by the whole human race, and He wants Himself to be known and worshiped. Therefore, He wills that there be public and honorable gatherings, and that in these the voice of the Gospel sound forth. He wants to be worshiped and celebrated there. (LC43: 146)

As he also spells out with some detail in his *Loci Communes*:

> We use the Lord's Supper as a sacrament inasfar as it is a testimony by which faith is guided. Secondly, this faith itself with the outward participation in the sacrament is a kind of sacrifice, because God pronounces that this faith, and exercises of this kind, in the New Testament are sacrifices of praise and a form of worship. Thus, this spiritual obedience itself becomes a kind of sacrifice by which honor is given to God which He requires and approves. Then, since with this faith there is of necessity joined the giving of thanks for the highest benefit which He has bestowed upon us and the church, thus it is called a *eucharistia* (a sacrifice of thanksgiving). Besides this there is also the need for confession; for we have shown that we believe the Gospel and should invite others to follow our example. All these things are eucharistic sacrifices. (LC43: 152)

Thus, Melanchthon maintains and recaptures the proper role of ceremony in worship. He certainly does not indicate that ceremony is wrong, nor even optional or unimportant. But the purpose and goal of Christian ceremony is that the merits and benefits of Christ are bestowed upon His faithful people. And of course, applying the merits of Christ to one's self by faith, or the *spiritual eating* of Christ, is an essential element of the daily sacrifice; indeed, it *is* the eucharistic sacrifice. Precisely as such, it is also necessary for the salutary use of the Sacrament. It is true that the spiritual eating of Christ by faith also occurs outside of the Lord's Supper, but by no means is the Sacramental eating superfluous. In point of fact, the Eucharist stands with the

Word proclaimed as one of the regular and constitutive elements of Christian worship. Preaching and the Sacrament belong together, and faith lays hold of Christ in both.[44]

> Therefore Paul says (I Cor. 11:26), "As often as you eat this bread and drink the cup, you proclaim the Lord's death." (Tappert: 256, Ap.XXIV [35])[45]

As Melanchthon had written earlier, in Ap.IV:

> The Lord's Supper was instituted in the church so that as this sign reminds us of the promises of Christ, the remembrance might strengthen our faith and announce the blessings of Christ. (Tappert: 136, Ap.IV [210])[46]

44 "What must be seen is that in the Lutheran Confessions as in the New Testament the Eucharist is not an occasional extra, an exceptional additive for especially pious occasions, but a regular, central and constitutive feature of Christian worship. Preaching and the Sacrament belong together not anyhow, or helter-skelter, by statistical coincidence, but as mutually corresponding elements within one integrated whole." (Marquart: 335)

45 Luther provides the following collect based on 1 Corinthians 11:26:

V. As often as ye eat this bread and drink this cup;

R. Ye shall show the Lord's death till he come.

O thou dear Lord God, who in connection with this wonderful sacrament hast commanded us to commemorate and preach thy passion: Grant that we may so use this sacrament of thy body and blood that daily and richly we may be conscious of they redemption. Amen. (LW 53:137 [1533])

46 Luther comments in his treatise, *Against the Heavenly Prophets*:

This remembrance of Christ is an outward remembrance, as one can speak of remembering any one.... By the words, "This do in remembrance of me," Christ meant what Paul meant by his words, "Proclaim the death of the Lord," etc. [I Cor. 11:26]. Christ wants us to make him known when we receive the sacrament and proclaim the gospel, so as to confirm faith....

From this you know well that such remembrance does not justify, but that they must first be justified who would preach, proclaim, and practice the outward remembrance of Christ, as it is written in Rom. 10[:10], "For man believes with his heart and so is justified, and he confesses with his

This remembrance of Christ is a eucharistic sacrifice, the very antithesis of the Roman Mass. As Melanchthon explains in Ap.XXIV:

> Although the ceremony is a memorial of the death of Christ, therefore, it is not the daily sacrifice by itself; the commemoration is the real daily sacrifice, the proclamation and the faith which truly believes that by the death of Christ God has been reconciled. There must be a drink offering, *i.e.*, the effect of the proclamation, as we are sanctified, put to death, and made alive when the Gospel sprinkles us with the blood of Christ. There must also be an offering in thanksgiving, confession, and affliction. (Tappert: 257, Ap.XXIV [38])

As we have seen, the eucharistic sacrifice includes many activities, but all have repentance and faith in common. All are "eucharistic," that is, a thanksgiving, since all are directed toward God in faith. All are a "sacrifice," that is, a death and offering, since all are directed away from ourselves; simultaneously, we are put to death with repentance, and offered to God by faith as we entrust ourselves to His care.[47]

---

lips and so is saved." (LW 40:208 [1525])

47 Melanchthon writes in his *Commentary on Romans* (12:1):

What is the emphasis in the word "sacrifices"? First, an offering is a certain confession or testimony that we acknowledge God. Sacrificing signifies that it is destined to death for sin, that this sinful nature must be destroyed, and that obedience must be rendered to God by that death. Therefore, he includes these three things when he mentions sacrifice: recognition or glorification of God; mortification of ourselves, or that obedience must be shown in such mortification; and faith, by which we believe that these sacrifices are pleasing to God on account of Christ, the sacrificial victim, to whom all sacrifices at all times pointed, and on account of whom they were accepted. Therefore the meaning is this: Become sacrifices, that is,

All of these activities do indeed take place in the proper use of the Lord's Supper. Thus, even though the Lord's Supper itself is *not* a sacrifice but rather a pure Sacrament and a gracious gift of God; yet, the celebration and reception of this Sacrament must be a "*Eucharist*," that is, a sacrifice of repentance, faith, and thanksgiving.

Let us now recall that Melanchthon includes *proclamation of the Gospel* first of all among the parts of the "real daily sacrifice." And not only is the Lord's Supper itself a proclamation; it is always accompanied by the public preaching of the Gospel. Laying hold of this proclamation is *the faith that truly believes* the promise offered and bestowed in the Lord's Supper. Such faith is the central part of the daily sacrifice, and by now it should be obvious that all of the Lutheran Reformers require faith for a salutary use of the Sacrament.[48]

Just because the ceremony is "useless" without faith, it should not be thought that faith could get along just fine without the external Word and Sacrament. As strongly as the Lutherans argued against the Roman "*ex opere operato*," which belittled the need for faith, so strongly did they also reject those who belittled the need for Sacraments. Indeed, Melanchthon describes the salutary use of the Sacrament

---

acknowledge, proclaim, or glorify God, and undergo mortification, and believe that these acts of your worship are pleasing to God on account of Christ, on account of whom you also are sacrifices. This is the very simple meaning. (*Romans*: 212)

48 "As the promise is useless unless faith accepts it, so the ceremony is useless without the faith which really believes that the forgiveness of sins is being offered here. Such a faith encourages the contrite mind." (Tappert: 262, Ap.XXIV [69])

specifically as *the* worship of the New Testament.[49] The problem is thus deeper and more profound than a simple, external choice between Rome and the fanatics.

With or without ceremony, people will always attempt to worship God in one of two ways:—either by sacrificing their own works to earn God's favor apart from the Cross, or by sacrificing themselves in response to God's favor in, with and under the Cross. Likewise, there are only two possible sacrifices with which to approach the Lord's Supper (and one or the other must be present, never both):—either by crucifying Christ again (to judgment), or by crucifying the self with Christ by faith (to salvation). Reception of the Lord's Supper should be a kind of prayer for grace and mercy. And as with prayer, so also with the Lord's Supper; the communicant approaches the Altar either with humble confidence in the forgiveness of Christ, or in reliance on his or her own works and worthiness. The first is a proper, eucharistic sacrifice; the latter, a return to the Roman sacrifice of the Mass. In the same way, it must be said, those who quickly tire of hearing about and receiving the Sacrament, and who instead demand more emphasis on "sanctification" and the third use of the Law, demonstrate a *de facto* return to Rome. Sooner or later, such people invariably have more regard for their own works than for the work of Christ.

Another essential aspect of the daily sacrifice is the dying of the Old Adam and the rising of the New Man, being

---

49 He writes in the Apology:

> This use of the sacrament, when faith gives life to terrified hearts, is the worship of the New Testament, because what matters in the New Testament is the spiritual motivation, dying and being made alive. (Tappert: 262, Ap.XXIV [71])

put to death and made alive. This daily dialectic is, of course, classic Lutheran theology:—the work of the Law and the Gospel, the significance of Baptism, the repentance and faith that constitute the Christian life, as already discussed above. Here, then, is where the concept of sacrifice is most helpful and should by all means be recaptured. As Luther prays in the Our Father paraphrase of his *Deutsche Messe*,"that we may be strengthened by his Spirit to do and to suffer his will . . . and always to break, slay, and sacrifice our own wills" (LW 53:79 [1526]).

The mortification of our flesh takes place through a participation in the Cross of Christ. Being united with His Body and His Blood as separate elements, *in, with, and under* the bread and wine, we participate not only in the Person of Christ as the Son of God; we receive Him precisely as the one, eternally-significant, Sacrificial Lamb of God, Who lives and reigns forever as the One Who has been slain (present perfect tense). "It is precisely this act of reception of Christ's sacrifice which is called sacrifice in the New Testament" (Koch: 171). And so, for example, no doubt with such thoughts in mind, Chemnitz writes in his treatise on *The Lord's Supper*:

> Some prayers of the ancient Greek fathers are extant in which with the sweetest words they say that the body and blood of Christ, when they are eaten by us in the Supper, become for us the "acceptable offering" (*euprosdektos apologia*) which we can bring before the tribunal of God [Rom. 15:16,31]. (Chemnitz, LS: 190)

All of these previous actions of the daily sacrifice — proclamation, faith, prayer, dying and rising — invariably lead to the final part, namely, *thanksgiving* or *eucharistia*. And because thanksgiving is where the true spiritual sacrifice always arrives, the "eucharistic sacrifice" is named from this one aspect. Likewise, in recognition that the daily sacrifice in all its parts does take place in the ceremony of the Lord's Supper, the Sacrament also has been given the name *Eucharist*. As Melanchthon describes:

> There is also a sacrifice [a thank–offering], since one action can have several purposes. Once faith has strengthened a conscience to see its liberation from terror, then it really gives thanks for the blessing of Christ's suffering. It uses the ceremony itself as praise to God, as a demonstration of its gratitude, and a witness of its high esteem for God's gifts. Thus the ceremony becomes a sacrifice of praise. (Tappert: 262, Ap.XXIV [74])[50]

---

50 Or, as Melanchthon writes in his *Loci Communes*:

> Of necessity for the strengthening of faith we need to add the next purpose [of the Sacrament], that is, the giving of thanks. Thus the name that is given to this ceremony is the Eucharist. For at this point in the teaching of this matter we must remember the benefits of Christ. In public proclamation and in our private prayers we must give clear expression of thanksgiving. (LC43:148)

To this end, Melanchthon continues with an appropriate example of Eucharistic Prayer, as different from the Canon of the Roman Mass as true eucharist always is from all attempts at self–propitiation. In the spirit of the Eastern Anaphorae, he prays:

> Almighty God, the eternal Father of our Lord Jesus Christ, Creator of all things and Preserver of them together with Your coeternal Son, our Lord Jesus Christ, and Your Holy Spirit, have mercy on me for the sake of Your Son, Jesus Christ. With marvelous wisdom and inerrant counsel You have willed Him to be made a sacrifice for us; and at the same time You have shown Your wrath against sin and Your immeasurable mercy toward the human race. Sanctify, guide, and aid me by Your Holy Spirit. Guide and preserve Your church and Your governments, which are protectors of the churches.

This act of thanksgiving — in the Lord's Supper and throughout the Christian life — is always a two-fold sacrifice. For even as we praise and give thanks for the works of God, we likewise renounce all our own works and efforts. Thus, the mutual sacrifice of praise and repentance can be broken in either one of two ways: "The sinner can despair over his sin. He examines himself without lifting his eyes to God and accepting his gifts. Such a man cannot praise God. He is lost, because even in the confession of his sins he clings to himself and thinks that he ought to effect rather than accept his righteousness. Or else he presumes to praise God without condemning himself. But as long as he continues in his sin, his song remains an empty show" (Vajta, *Luther on Worship*: 157–158). In the words of Melanchthon:

> I give You thanks, Almighty God, eternal Father of our Lord Jesus Christ, Creator and Preserver of all things, together with Your coeternal Son, our Lord Jesus Christ, and Your Holy Spirit, that in Your immeasurable goodness You have revealed to Your church also Your Son, our Lord Jesus Christ, that He might be made a sacrifice for us and that through him there is given to us the remission of sins and life everlasting. You bestow these great blessings of Yours to us through the Gospel and Sacraments. You preserve the church and the ministry of the Gospel, and do not allow them to be destroyed. God, grant that we may be able to consider and celebrate with grateful and burning hearts this great goodness of Yours and the enormous benefits. But I pray that You would raise us up by Your Holy Spirit, so that our minds may be truly grateful and that gratitude may shine forth in our lives, etc.
>
> To you also, O Jesus Christ, Son of God, crucified and raised for us, I give thanks that in Your great love for us You have interceded with the eternal Father for the human race and have been made a sacrificial victim for us and have drawn down upon Yourself the wrath of God toward our sins. Kindle our hearts so that we may rejoice in true gratitude for Your enormous benefit, which is beyond our understanding, etc. (LC43: 148)

> As I have said, the true sacrifices of which God approves are to ask him for help and to give him thanks for the benefits that you have received [Ps. 50:14f.]. Now thanksgiving is truly to realize that the good thing you have received comes from God, and then to proclaim and publicly confess that God has helped you, so that others too may learn to trust God and to glorify him. (*Colossians*: 106)

Conclusion

As the royal priests of God, we enter the Holy of Holies with all boldness and confidence through the flesh and blood of Christ; and entering, we offer a sacrifice in the presence of God. Now, in what does our sacrifice consist? Certainly *not* some portion of our property, nor some token from our lives, designed to buy God's favor or otherwise pay Him off. We do not pay, as it were, some manner of spiritual "protection money" to a heavenly Crime Lord; nor do we bribe the Father to bless a life that remains, for all intents and purposes, our own. Rather, in receiving the Body and Blood of Christ, we sacrifice nothing less than ourselves. We sacrifice our pride, our self–confidence, our self–preservation; we sacrifice our Old Adam. We purposefully and intentionally repeat the significance of our Baptism, in which our Old Adam is drowned and destroyed, that the New Man Who is Christ may take our life entirely to be His own. We publicly confess our faith and confidence in God our heavenly Father, and what is more, we physically commit our bodies and souls and all things into His hands.

We make this sacrifice of ourselves with no thought

or pretension that we are worthy of ourselves to stand before God or offer anything to Him. Quite to the contrary, we commit ourselves to His care in and through Christ alone. We enter the Holy of Holies in repentance and in faith, acknowledging our complete lack of worthiness and our total dependance on God's mercy and forgiveness in Christ. We stake our very lives upon the certainty of His Sacrifice upon the Altar of the Cross, by which an eternal Atonement has been established once for all. On that basis alone, we sacrifice ourselves with Christ. We participate in His crucified Body and shed Blood. We take up His Cross and follow Him. We are, as St. Paul writes, crucified with Him. We do, in fact, as Jesus says to James and John, drink the Cup that He has drunk; we are "baptized" with His Blood in the Baptism of His Cross. We are nourished by the Body that lived and died for us, thereby consecrating and sacrificing our own bodies to Christ alone, to the glory of His Name and for the good of our neighbors. The Sacrifice of Christ is finished and complete — offered once for all upon the Cross and never to be repeated or replaced. Now, on the basis of His Sacrifice, the fruits of which we receive entirely as a gift in the Lord's Supper, we enter the Holy of Holies with thanksgiving and sacrifice ourselves to God in Christ.

But where do we go from here? Obviously, the eucharistic sacrifice is not confined to a godly use of the Sacrament. The Christian who approaches the Eucharist with repentant faith and thanksgiving, likewise leaves in faith — and with his or her faith renewed — to live the entire spectrum of life in sacrificial praise to God. "To offer oneself to God is simultaneously to turn to one's neighbor in a concrete, totally human manner" (Koch: 174). Thus, we conclude with some brief comments on the movement of the eucharistic sacrifice from the Altar of Christ into the daily activity of those who no longer live for themselves but for Him who for their sake died and was raised.

Part of the genius behind the Lord's Supper is the *earthiness* of its elements and actions. As with all the Means of Grace, God approaches us on the level of our flesh and blood, even as the *Word became flesh and dwelt among us.* Thus God lays hold of us, and allows us to lay hold of Him, in such a way that faith involves not only the heart by itself but also the body — the eyes and ears, the hands and feet. The *communio* created in the Lord's Supper is therefore not only a"spiritual" matter, but a matter of *body and soul.*[51] Participation in the Eucharist necessarily transforms the faith of our heart into a faith that is active in, with, and under the actions of our flesh. The hand that reaches out in faith to take the Body and Blood of Christ will likewise reach out by faith to the neighbor; the mouth that eats in faith will likewise speak the faith, as St. Paul indicates in Romans 10:10,"With the heart man believes . . . and with the mouth he confesses." Just as faith is strengthened in the Lord's Supper, so is the body prepared by the Body of Christ for all manner of good works and for the eucharistic sacrifice of a Christian life.

---

51 With this *communio* in mind, Melanchthon writes of the responsibility that Christians have toward one another:

> With this common participation we obligate ourselves to manifest friendship, love, fidelity, and helpfulness to one another as members of one Lord and Savior, *Jesus Christ.* Of this obligation Paul also speaks,"Because we all partake of one bread, we are one body" [I Cor. 10:17]. After participation, therefore, whoever offends another's conscience offends the body and blood of Christ. (LC55: 219)

For Luther and Melanchthon, and for those who follow in their train, there is always a close connection between the eucharistic liturgy and the eucharistic life. The Christian is continuously recreated and nourished in the "Sacrament of love." Thus the eucharistic sacrifice that begins by receiving the gifts of God in faith continues in the sacrifice of love, which believers offer to one another. *Worship* is not confined to the pious exercises of the liturgy. That is where it begins, to be sure, in the service of God (*Gottesdienst*). But from there it entails "the whole of Christian life in service and self-surrender to the needs of the world. Our stewardship and offering of material gifts retain their close relation to the liturgy. But they are vastly more than a liturgical act. The latter might be a mere fragment, a work of merit, brought forward to obtain the grace of God. But true bodily sacrifice is a total, continued giving of self which includes both faith and action" (Vajta, *Luther on Worship*: 169).

There is certainly a sense of this movement from faithful reception to active love, for example, in Luther's "Christian Questions and Answers ... for Those Who Intend to Go to the Sacrament":

> Finally, why do you wish to go to the Sacrament?
> That I may learn to believe that Christ died for my sin out of great love ... and that I may also learn of Him to love God and my neighbor. (*Lutheran Worship*: 306–307)

Which is to say, finally, "we receive [the Lord's Supper] not only — in the words of the familiar Lutheran post-communion collect — that through it God might strengthen us individually in faith toward him, but also that he might by it increase our fervent love toward one another."[52]

---

52 Piepkorn, "Christ Today: His Presence in the Sacraments," *Lutheran World* 10 (July 1963): 283

Partial Bibliography of Primary Sources

Tappert, Theodore G., General Editor. *The Book of Concord: The Confessions of the Evangelical Lutheran Church*. Translated and edited by Th. Tappert, Jaroslav Pelikan, Robert H. Fischer, and Arthur C. Piepkorn. Philadelphia, PA: Fortress Press, 1959; Twelfth Printing, 1978.

Melanchthon, Philip

1521. *Propositions on the Mass*. Translated from the Latin by Charles Leander Hill. In *Melanchthon: Selected Writings*, ed. Elmer Ellsworth Flack and Lowell J. Satre (Minneapolis, MN: Augsburg Publishing House, 1962): 62–67.

1521. *Annotations on the First Epistle to the Corinthians*. Introduced, Translated, and Edited by John Patrick Donnelly. Milwaukee: Marquette University Press, 1995.

1527. *Paul's Letter to the Colossians*. Translated by David C. Parker. Ahmond: 1989.

1530. *The Augsburg Confession*. Tappert: 23–96. [Concordia Triglotta: 37–95]

1531. *Apology of the Augsburg Confession*. Tappert: 97–285. [Concordia Triglotta: 97–451]

1540. *Commentary on Romans*. Translated by Fred Kramer. St. Louis, MO: Concordia Publishing House, 1992.

1543. *Loci Communes*. Translated from the Latin by J. A. O. Preus. St. Louis, MO: Concordia Publishing House, 1992.

1555. *Melanchthon on Christian Doctrine: Loci Communes*. Translated and edited by Clyde L. Manschreck. New York, NY: Oxford University Press, 1965.

www.ingramcontent.com/pod-product-compliance
Lightning Source LLC
Chambersburg PA
CBHW060053050426
42448CB00011B/2436

* 9 7 8 1 8 9 1 4 6 9 3 3 6 *